The 7 Laws of Influence

How to Influence People through Communication Skills, Body Language, Social Influence and Persuasion

FREE BONUS E-BOOK!

Get Success Results:

220 Principles That the Successful Use to Become Wildly Successful and How You Can Too

Learn the secrets and habits of the most successful people in the world and how you too can develop the right habits for success so you can live the life you've always wanted…

http://shapleighpublishing.com/GetSuccessResultsEbook/

© **Copyright 2016 by Brian Cagneey - All rights reserved.**

This document is geared towards providing exact and reliable information in regards to the topic and issue covered. The publication is sold with the idea that the publisher is not required to render accounting, officially permitted, or otherwise, qualified services. If advice is necessary, legal or professional, a practiced individual in the profession should be ordered.

- From a Declaration of Principles which was accepted and approved equally by a Committee of the American Bar Association and a Committee of Publishers and Associations.

In no way is it legal to reproduce, duplicate, or transmit any part of this document in either electronic means or in printed format. Recording of this publication is strictly prohibited and any storage of this document is not allowed unless with written permission from the publisher. All rights reserved.

The information provided herein is stated to be truthful and consistent, in that any liability, in terms of inattention or otherwise, by any usage or abuse of any policies, processes, or directions contained within is the solitary and utter responsibility of the recipient reader. Under no circumstances will any legal responsibility or blame be held against the publisher for any reparation, damages, or monetary loss due to the information herein, either directly or indirectly.

Respective authors own all copyrights not held by the publisher.

The information herein is offered for informational purposes solely, and is universal as so. The presentation of the information is without contract or any type of guarantee assurance.

The trademarks that are used are without any consent, and the publication of the trademark is without permission or backing by the trademark owner. All trademarks and brands within this book are for clarifying purposes only and are the owned by the owners themselves, not affiliated with this document.

Table Of Contents

FREE BONUS E-BOOK! 1

INTRODUCTION: WHAT DOES INFLUENCE REALLY MEAN? ... 4

CHAPTER 1: THE FIRST LAW OF INFLUENCE - THE SINGLE IDEA OF INFLUENCE THAT CAN CHANGE SOMEONE'S LIFE ... 7

CHAPTER 2: THE SECOND LAW- FOCUS ON THESE AREAS TO HAVE MORE INFLUENCE 16

CHAPTER 3: THE THIRD LAW- 5 BASIC PRINCIPLES OF INFLUENCE 23

CHAPTER 4: THE FOURTH LAW- SIMPLE BODY LANGUAGE SIGNS THAT INFLUENCE 29

CHAPTER 5: THE FIFTH LAW- THE COMMUNICATION SKILLS NEEDED TO INFLUENCE 34

CHAPTER 6: THE SIXTH LAW- HOW TO INFLUENCE WITHOUT WORDS 40

CHAPTER 7: THE SEVENTH LAW- THE KEYS TO POSITIVE PERSUASION 43

CONCLUSION 49

FREE BONUS E-BOOK! 50

OTHER BOOKS IN THE "7 LAWS" SERIES 51

Introduction: What does Influence Really Mean?

I want to thank you and congratulate you for purchasing the book, *"The 7 Laws of Influence"*.

This book contains proven steps and strategies on how to improve your ability to influence those around you. In order to get to that, we should first define what the word influence really means.

Influence, a Simple Definition:

Regardless of the level of material that has been published on the subject of influence, both online and in traditional print, many people have a hard time precisely defining the word. Influence refers to the power or act of bringing an effect to life using a low level of force or a simple display of command. It also refers to the capacity of power to cause reactions or effects in a way that is intangible or indirect. Based on these definitions of the term, it's obvious that having influence means effecting external circumstances in life.

The remaining question here, then, is what changes are being brought about, and what is being changed. When it comes to social media or businesses, what is being changed is nearly always either a person or multiple people. When it comes to what is being changed, however, this can mean many different things. It can refer to a mental change, such as a shift in attitude, opinion, or sentiment. On the other hand, it could be a change in action, like behavior alterations, referrals, or a purchase. Does this mean that, in order to have influence, action must be involved?

Does Influence always Include Action?

Contrary to what many believe, no, it does not have to lead to an action. If you have changed someone's mind about their favorite sports team, you have still had influence, even if they haven't done anything differently. Some would argue that influence that doesn't lead to action is not very valuable, but it's still technically influence, and can lead to action. It would seem, then, that influence is simply the capacity to bring about a shift in one's actions or thoughts. But this definition does not cover the most important aspect of true influence.

The Means Matter as Much as the End:

The above definition for influence is not complete, because the ways in which you make those changes occur, either in action or thought, matter a lot. The classic definition of influence also claims that no overt command or force should be necessary, and that any shifts in action or thought should be brought about using intangible or indirect methods. So, what can be taken from this idea? To put it simply, the means for influence matter just as much as the end result. In essence, influence has to come along with integrity.

Mind-Changing Methods without Integrity:

It isn't very difficult to alter someone's actions or thoughts, since many options exist for how to do it. Here are some basic ways to change someone's mind:

- **Bribery or Paying:** This can be seen as the "carrot" method, because you are urging someone along with the promise of reward. This means that the influence is not truly genuine. If it were, no bribe would have been necessary in the first place.

- **Force or Fear:** This method relies on coercion, control, or command, and plays on negative factors in order to influence a person. Again, this doesn't possess the level of respect necessary for a beneficial, influential relationship.

- **Pressure or Annoyance:** This can also be considered pestering someone until they give in. An example of this method would be online spam.

- **Deception:** Another method for influence is deception, and applies to anything that uses tricks to get something done, or has a hidden agenda. If the person you are influencing cannot know what your true intentions or reasons are, it's not influence with integrity.

None of the above are actual influence. It's true that threatening a person often works for changing their behavior or mind, but that's a different story and does not count as real influence. Paying a person to do you a favor is also a method for changing their mind or actions, but also does not count as true influence. The above paragraphs should make clear that it's more difficult to really influence a person than to simply convince them to do something for you. What this means is that influence is being able to change someone's actions or thoughts using transparent, non-forceful methods, where the person being influenced actually wants the changes, voluntarily and free of bribery.

How to Apply this Definition of Influence:

We have now defined influence explicitly, so it's time to try applying it to make it even clearer. If you take a look at scoring algorithms or models for influence, you will probably come upon a few questions. Should, for example, the amount of followers a person has on Facebook play a role in their level of influence? While some may say no, others may see a different side of the story. In reality, it depends on how they got those followers. Some people pay others to follow them on social media, and this does not quality as real influence. However, gaining followers naturally based on what you post would be real, genuine influence.

Influence does not just apply to being able to cause changes in actions or thoughts, because the way you make these changes happen is important. Instead of assuming that influence can only happen through bribery or dishonest means, it's time to see how to genuinely gain more influence and success in your life.

Thanks again for purchasing this book, I hope you enjoy it!

Chapter 1: The First Law of Influence - The Single Idea of Influence that can Change Someone's Life

Influence refers to the act of applying power with the intention of a specific goal in mind. Studies show that the average person usually attempts to influence or lead others by using specific positive techniques. These are modeling, appealing to morals or values, building an alliance, consulting for advice, appealing to a relationship, social interactions, stating, trading, legitimizing, or persuading with logic. Plenty of negative tactics exist for influence as well, including threats, manipulation, avoidance, and intimidation. We will go over these tactics in detail, but first, let's cover the first law of influence.

The 1st Law of Influence: The Single Idea of Influence That Can Change Someone's Life

Everyone has influence. Before you were born you had influence, and after you die you'll have it. Everything from the tone of voice we use, to the words we say, to the body language we have, affects our level of influence over others. From political negotiations between superpower nations, to the kind extending of a warm hand, influence is everywhere. We have already covered some of the basics about influence, such as it meaning the ability to change someone or something, or the power to cause changes without directly forcing them to happen. But what else does this word refer to?

- **Deciding where to Add Value:** Those definitions play themselves out in a simple idea: Influence is all about determining how and who to add value to. Influence is about adding something important and positive to someone else's life.

- **Putting the Needs of Others First:** People often think of influence in a selfish way, such as asking themselves how they can get others to do what they want, but there is another way to view this idea.. Influence is determined by how abundantly you place others needs first.

- **Positivity truly Matters:** The more positive your interactions with another person or circumstance, the higher level of influence you will have. Although negative coercion can work for influencing someone, it is not a lasting or significant method, since they didn't choose it on their own.

- **How Influence relates to Giving:** To increase your influence you have to become a giver. Because everyone naturally thinks of themselves first, increasing your influence and becoming a giver will mean you have to change in a positive way to start focusing on others. If people sense that you are selfless and truly concerned about others, influence comes naturally and people will be enthusiastic to follow you.

In addition to these personal approaches to influence, the word can also refer to complex alliances, such as those between countries. It can also be the simple smile you receive from a stranger on the subway. Each time a person attempts to change the way others decide, behave, or think, they are attempting to exercise influence over them. Handshakes and smiles are the attempts of forming connections, socializing, and getting rid of barriers. The more a person gets to know you and likes you, the more likely they will be to do what you want them to do. Let's go over some basic influencing tactics.

Rational Methods for Exercising Influence:

- **Modeling:** Modeling refers to acting in specific ways that you wish for others to emulate. This refers to coaching, mentoring, teaching, or being a role model. This also refers to being able to influence others without even realizing that y9ou're doing it. Managers, important public faces, and leaders use this model very often, and sometimes it's intentional, while other times it isn't.

- **Appealing to Morals or Values:** This is a method for influence that is emotional, or attempts to appeal to the feelings of another person. This is a main way that others become influenced or a method to influence multiple people at one time. This method is a surefire way to gain true commitment from people, and is used often by politicians, idealists, leaders, fundraisers, and spiritual or religious figures. A person being emotionally invested in your idea is the best way to gain true influence.

- **Building an Alliance:** Looking for support or building an alliance can be used to influence people. This method isn't used very often, but involves gaining agreement or cooperation using group or peer pressure. Although this method isn't as common as some of the other methods, in some situations, it's the only way to exercise influence.

- **Consulting for Advice:** This refers to stimulating or engaging people by using questions, and getting them involved with the solution or issue at hand. Asking someone questions about something automatically makes them feel like a part of the situation, meaning that they become mentally invested. This is known as a power tool in the world of influence, and works best when used by confident, socially intelligent people who have a desire to share ideas.

- **Appealing to a Relationship:** This refers to gaining cooperation or agreement from a person that you are already familiar with, and how well it works depends on how long you have known the person and how close you are. Examples of this method would be asking a friend for a favor in a tough situation and knowing that you can rely on the relationship.

- **Social Interactions:** This method of influence involves taking a personal interest in the other individual, being friendly and open, and searching for common interests to talk about. This could also involve giving others compliments intended to lift them up and make them feel nice. Even people who aren't aware of the concept of influence use this without realizing it. In many situations and cultures across the world, this technique is necessary and useful.

- **Stating:** This refers to simply asserting whatever it is you want or believe, and is used as a strong power tool for influencing others. This works best when the person talking states their ideas in a self-confident and authoritative voice. Striking a balance is important here, since resistance can result from trying to use too much force and have the opposite of the desired effect.

- **Trading:** This involves exchanging or negotiating in an attempt to gain cooperation or involvement. This works the best when you use implicit methods, instead of explicit. Although this method is not as common as some of the others, there are situations where it is the only technique that will work.

- **Legitimizing:** This method refers to the appeal to those in authority. Usually, this is one of the less effective techniques for influencing. However, this tool does work for some, and can also result in fast cooperation or compliance.

- **Persuading with Logic:** This method is pretty straightforward, and refers to the use of logic to talk about what you want or believe. This technique is the most popular of all influencing tools across the globe, and is used most often in most cultures. It's important to note, however, that this technique doesn't work for all people and may be inappropriate in certain circumstances.

Now that we've gone over some of the most commonly used and basic methods for influence (both on a personal and professional scale), we can review some of the more negative tactics used to influence. The essence of these tactics is getting others to do something that they don't want to do or would not have voluntarily agreed to. These go against integrity and are what should be avoided when it comes to the subject of influence.

Negative Tactics for Exercising Influence:

- **Coercion Tactics:** Instead of using the constructive tactics described in the last section, some people use their positions of power to get people to follow their orders. This is what is called coercion, and means that the colleagues or family likely will not enjoy the task that they have been coerced into. This means that if the task is difficult they could just give up on it. This will lead to more coercion and orders, in an attempt to save the idea, but could end up unsuccessful, since the people involved are more or less being forced into it, not participating by choice.

- **Nagging Tactics:** Everyone knows that one person who thinks the best way to influence or persuade others is by constantly talking. They believe that this will lead them to gaining involvement and cooperation from others, and thus repeat their opinions or ideas over and over again. Another word for this act is nagging. This works as an influence tactic, at times, because people end up giving in as a way to get the person to stop bothering them. However in general, people who were persuaded by being nagged likely have not actually committed to the idea enthusiastically. For this reason, influence gained by this method can never be as genuine as influence gained by real methods.

- **Threats:** This refers to threats either on an implicit or explicit level. For instance, a boss may ask their best employee to come in on a Saturday, and hint at the fact that they will lose their position if they don't comply. Obviously, this type of persuasion and influence can very easily cause resentment and negativity. The support gained by using threats will also be less genuine, and may even be based solely on fear, which is a poisonous factor in any relationship, personal or professional.

- **Avoidance:** Trying to avoid your responsibilities by forcing other people to do your work for you (regardless of what benefits them) is a negative form of influence. A common and relatable example of this would be a boss trying to slack off on their responsibilities by giving his employees more work to do. This type of behavior does nothing to foster healthy working relationships or quality rapport. In addition to this, acting in an indirect or passive aggressive manner is another form of trying to exert influence in a negative way.

- **Intimidation or Bullying:** When you impose yourself on other people by making them comply, this is a negative influencing tactic. This includes being insensitive, aloof, arrogant, overbearing, or just plain loud. These are the techniques used by bullies who do not treat others as individuals worthy of respect. Although this may work for getting someone to do your bidding, it isn't the healthy way to approach any subject.

The methods listed above are not good methods, for obvious reasons. People only use them when they don't know what else to do, but better ways always exist. This means that the best way to persuade another person is to convince them to believe in your idea or vision. Someone being aware that they are being forcefully influenced will almost never appreciate it.

Persuasion and How it Relates to Influence:

How many times in your life have you wanted to persuade a person into something? This is a common situation that comes up all the time, in the form of convincing your son to get out of bed in time for school, or a friend to take notes for you in the class you won't be able to make it to. For some, this seems to come naturally, without others even noticing what they're doing, but for others, using positions of power is necessary to get what they need done. The skill of persuasion can be developed, the way other skills can be developed, and is necessary for having influence.

What Prevents Effective Persuasion?

To begin thinking about the subject of persuasion, it's helpful to first think about what doesn't work for persuading others. Here are some common obstacles that stand in the way of productive persuasion:

- **Overconfidence:** Assuming that you are much better with persuasion than you actually are can be a detriment to the level of influence you will have. This state of mind assumes that you already know everything you need to know and have no need to improve your skills. Instead of falling into this trap, make sure that you are evaluating yourself regularly and honestly and figuring out where you can improve.

- **Being too Keen:** When someone comes across as trying very hard to be persuasive, it often has the opposite effect. When a person is overly enthusiastic, it can close them off to suggestions from other people, or alternative creative methods. In addition to this, desperation will turn people off from being effectively persuaded, and can be spotted from a mile away.

- **Being against Real Effort:** No goal is possible if you don't put in the necessary effort to make it happen. Some people may try to use influence or persuasion to avoid work, by getting others to do it for them. This will not work in the long run.

- **Forgetting to Listen:** Nothing will hold you back from being effective at persuading others than talking often, but forgetting to listen. In a similar vein, giving far too much info will just leave people confused. Remember, as you have conversations, that it should be a two-way street.

- **Fearing Rejection:** Being too caught up in the fear of rejection can contribute to being bad at persuasion. People can sense the vibe or idea you are holding about yourself, and being fearful of rejection is very off-putting to a person you are attempting to persuade or influence.

- **Being Unprepared**: Although "winging it" can be effective in some situations, it doesn't always work. Oftentimes, people will see through this method and assume that you think your time is more valuable than their time. For this reason, being fully prepared in every situation is the best way to be truly influential and persuasive.

- **Assuming**: Another roadblock to having influence is assuming facts about people. This causes a form of blindness and limits creativity. In order to be truly persuasive, you should always remain open and receptive to your audience, making adjustments as necessary when new facts emerge.

Now that we have reviewed some roadblocks to being a persuasive and influential person, we can get down to persuasion tactics that are successful. Studies have shown that there are multiple traits and skills that people appreciate in influential characters.

Key Traits and Skills in Persuasive and Influential People:

Studies suggest that the elements of persuasion rely heavily on emotions. This means the ability to:

- **Honesty:** Keep your promises. You never make an agreement that you cannot live up to, and speak with integrity and respect at all times.

- **Personal Responsibility:** Take responsibility for yourself. You never blame others for your shortcomings and are focused on solutions when problems arise.

- **Reliability:** Be reliable, honest, genuine, and sincere. You always show up when you say you will and people know that they can count on you.

- **Knowledge:** You should also intimately know your subject, and believe in it fully. No one can have influence if they don't believe in what they're doing. Sincerity and enthusiasm goes a long way when it comes to persuasion and influence over others.

- **Charisma:** You must know how to be entertaining and build rapport, and stay away from arguments. An influential person has tact in conversation and is self-aware when it comes to disagreements.

- **Confidence**: Another key aspect here is self-confidence. This means having a healthy sense of self-esteem and a high level of emotional intelligence. You know that you are capable of succeeding, and usually do, as a result.

- **Motivation**: It's also important to stay motivated with your ideas and have a firm, strong belief for your capabilities.

- **Effective Communication**: Skills of communication are highly important for influential people. You need to know how to get your idea across in an effective and succinct manner, or you will never influence anyone, no matter how good your idea may be.

- **Organization**: The last important skill for an influential person is personal organization. This includes always doing your research, being aware of your audience and the subject at hand. Taking the time to carefully consider your goals, and get them organized.

As you can see, there are many skills that come along with being a successful persuader. This means that the most important traits when it comes to successful influence are quite varied. Another important factor to remain aware of is knowing how people think and working with, rather than against, it.

Skills for Understanding your Audience:

A crucial element for persuasion is being aware of the way your audience reasons and thinks. This should involve the ability to thoroughly listen, and empathy. For someone who really listens, their audience will likely tell them what they really believe. This also goes a long way for rapport-building, since people can't help but like a person who is personally interested in them. The fact is that people are a lot more willing and excited about doing favors for someone if they consider them a friend. The idea matters less than the relationship between the two people.

Chapter 2: The Second Law- Focus on These Areas to have More Influence

Now that we've reviewed what influence means and some different tactics to use and avoid when it comes to persuasion, we should go over some more key factors to keep in mind.

The 2nd Law of Influence: Focus On These Areas to Have More Influence

- **Character**: You attract who you are like. To increase influence you need to increase your character and integrity. You can increase your character and integrity simply by following through on what you say you will do. Never, ever make an agreement to do something unless you are 100 percent sure you can live up to what you said. This means you must do what is right even when it is hard. To be influential, your word is your strongest asset.

- **Relationships**: As we mentioned earlier, people are much more likely to do favors for someone or be influenced by them if they feel favorable about that person. In other words, the deeper the relationship, the deeper the influence. Instead of simply seeing others as pawns that you wish to influence or persuade, you should make an attempt to know them on a real, personal level. This will cause them to respond more favorably to your request.

- **Knowledge**: It's not *only* about what you know, but you need to be competent to create confidence from others. If someone can sense that you speaking about a subject that you haven't taken the time to thoroughly research, they are less likely to believe in you or get enthusiastic about your ideas. Take the time to study what it is you care about, and others will respond to this, making you more influential in life.

- **Intuition**: Intuition all comes down to being in touch with what you feel. Good intuition will affect the intangibles like energy, morale, momentum and how you time your actions. People cannot help but trust a person who has finely honed skills of intuition, so work on listening to yours more. Intuition is like a muscle, the more you pay attention to it and work it, the stronger it will become.

- **Your Past Experience**: The mistakes you've made and the challenges you have overcome will go a long way in how you can influence others because it will help you relate to others that are going through something you have gone through. Also will make you more relatable and likeable because people will know you've struggled. It shows your humanity, you're not perfect and no one has to put you on a pedestal.

- **Past Success:** You need to have a track record that shows you have been successful in making your vision a reality. The mistakes and challenges are not as important as having past success that can give others confidence. This doesn't mean that if you haven't been successful yet, you don't have a chance. It simply means that showcasing your past success will go a long way in building confidence, and the belief others have in your abilities.

- **Ability**: You have to combine your knowledge and past success to showcase your ability. This also creates confidence from others. It is also about using your ability to go above and beyond the expectations of those you are influencing. This will strengthen your influence with others.

The Importance of Consistency in Influence:

A person who wants to be seen as respected and influential should always try to stay as consistent as possible in their actions, declarations, and attitudes. If you ever agree to a task or take a certain position on a subject, you must be consistent. This means that you can get agreement for something reasonable or innocuous, and then move onto more favors. This is what influence is all about, and being consistent allows for this, since people grow to respond favorably to your requests.

Relationship Building for Influence:

In order to be an influential person, it's important to pay attention to the relationships you build and their quality. Developing goodwill from others is probably the most important aspect of persuasion, and this centers on:

- **Searching for Ways to Help:** Asking yourself how you can be of value to others. People know it when you're only seeing them as a means to an end. To build truly genuine relationships with mutual influence, you should find ways to add value to their life, as well.

- **Reasonable Favors**: To be influential, the requests you make to other people should be reasonable, and you should be perceived as a competent task. You should also overtly care about the business or relationship you're involved in.

- **True Credibility**: Credibility also matters for influence, meaning that everyone knows you are always working for the common good, and finding solutions that benefit all people involved. You must be obviously concerned for the good of everyone and not only selfishly concerned.

The Importance of Reciprocation in Influence:

To be an effective persuader, you should remember that it's all about exchanging value. You should have in mind something valuable to bring to the table that can be traded for something of value from another person. To do a favor for someone usually implies that they should also return the favor when the time is right.

- **What can you Offer?** In order to enjoy successful outcomes, you should find out what you can bring to the table. In addition to this, search for the best way to present your idea or contribution. It's not all about what you can gain from others, and you should always be searching for new ways to bring more to the table.

- **The Art of Repaying:** In most cultures across the world, it is the norm to try to repay someone for doing something for you. This tactic is used widely in businesses in order to gain involvement and cooperation from individuals or groups. This simple fact of interpersonal dynamics is one of the reasons that influence is always present, whether you are aware of it or not.

- **Flexibility:** You must remain flexible in your requests, meaning that you can adjust when necessary based on the response you receive to your request. It's much more likely that you will find a working solution to an issue if you remain open to changes.

The Importance of Liking in Persuasion and Influence:

As we've mentioned a few times already, it's been proven that people are more willing to say yes to individuals that they feel favorable towards, than those they do not. The next logical question, then, is what traits make a person more likeable?

- **Physical Appearance:** Taking pride in the way you look will go a long way to increase your likeability. Of course, looks aren't everything, but being clean and well-groomed is helpful for personal interactions.

- **Common Interests:** People are more likely to feel favorable toward someone who shares traits in common with them, even if it's just the same first name.

- **Familiarity:** Familiarity increases likeability, meaning that the more you're around someone, the more of a chance there is to "grow on" them. In order to improve your relationship with a person, either professionally or personally, make sure you spend plenty of time around them.

- **Compliments:** Studies show that people like others who compliment them, because it increases their confidence and shows positive feelings. Make sure that these are genuine, however, because if someone seems fake it can have the opposite effect.

- **Cooperation:** Cooperating with someone or simply working together with them on a task (however small) can enhance positive behaviors and feelings. Start small with agreeing with the person and also looking for ways you can do them favors or work together.

Keeping all of the above factors in mind, you can work to improve and develop rapport with people, even if this area was not previously your strongest point. Although people may not be very open to suggestions at first, socializing with them and making an effort to get to know the real them will make them a lot more receptive. You will find that they are more open to your ideas once you make this effort.

The Role of Authority in Influence:

Basic rules of authority reveal that individuals usually defer to people who hold power positions. This can mean positions of leadership in general, specialized knowledge, great credentials, or an assertive and confident demeanor. In addition to this, we may be influenced to think of someone as authoritative based on their knowledge, clothes, or titles. You may notice that when a person is introduced to speak, they always have their credentials announced prior to this, resulting in a more favorable reception by the audience.

- **Credibility:** Although authority is useful for influence, credibility should be more desirable. In addition to developing your authority, also increase your credibility by utilizing your trustworthiness and also your expertise.

- **Trustworthiness:** Being trustworthy is the most important factor to building your authority and credibility. People will automatically trust you more if they are aware of your intentions and fully trust them. To become a trusted person, you have to actually believe in your own ideas.

How Validation on a Social Level Impacts Influence:

When a person doesn't know what they should do next, it's common that they will see what others are doing to get ideas. This concept is validation on a social level, and everyone looks for ideas by looking to others to see what is accepted. For this reason, explaining your intentions to people ahead of time can help with gaining agreement or cooperation from others. Once they are aware of where you're coming from, they are more likely to agree or say yes to your requests.

The Concept of Scarcity in Influence:

The idea of competing for resources that are limited in number is a powerful tool for motivation. In combination with a time constraint, this is even more beneficial. The result of the idea of scarcity on the way humans judge things, in general, is proven when someone who wants to purchase a home is undecided. When the realtor lets them know that another person is offering to buy the property with cash up front, the undecided person will feel a sense of urgency for making their purchase. This may lead them to respond more quickly than would have had their not been a sense of urgency. For this reason, the concept of scarcity is helpful for influencing or persuading others.

Which Potential Barriers stand in the Way of Influence?

As long as the relationship between two people (or a group of people) is there, achieving a task might be as simple as requesting that it get done. Other times, however, it isn't that simple. This is where having a level of influence comes in handy. Some common barriers to effective influence are:

- **No Common Ground:** In order for someone to be effectively influenced in a genuine way, they have to share a common vision with the influencer, at least to some degree. Without this, influence cannot truly take place.

- **No Adequate Incentive:** For some people who you are attempting to influence, an incentive might be necessary. A barrier exists when you don't have the means to provide this. However, with genuine influence that doesn't require coercion, an incentive isn't always necessary.

- **No Common Priorities or Goals:** For people to work together, they must share a common goal or priorities. In other words, they must have a similar enough vision to work together on a project or idea.

It's helpful to do some self-reflection to find which potential barriers might exist inside of you for being an effective influencer. This could be anything from being unprepared, to getting discouraged too fast, not having enough knowledge about influence, or having trouble coming up with creative new approaches to try. Persevering, in this case, will definitely pay off in the long run. Getting too caught up on the possibility of rejection can also slow down your path to success in influence.

The Importance of the Art of Persuasion in Business:

Our increasingly competitive world, with its growing and expanding business places, makes the need for smart and efficient employees all the more important. In other words, people who can resolve problems fast and negotiate with finesse are in increasingly high demand. Knowing the art of persuasion and influence is a necessary and powerful part of the modern professional world. For this principal to be even more beneficial, you should use this art to achieve tasks and carry out goals. To master influence is to master your life, and everything in it.

Chapter 3: The Third Law- 5 Basic Principles of Influence

The average person might consider influence as part of a relationship between someone in a superior position and someone in a lower position. However, someone who truly understands the art of influence knows that that is not the case. It's just as much about giving as it is about benefiting yourself. Let's take a look at the third law of influence.

The 3rd Law of Influence: 5 Basic Principles of Influence

- **Giving and Receiving:** In order to expect favors or cooperation from others, you have to have a giving mentality. People feel indebted to someone when they do something for them. This is not to be used as a manipulation technique. To have the true value of reciprocation *you* have to give first. Again, influence is about adding value, and that adding value has to come from you first. Initiative and a willing heart to give are the focus that makes reciprocation possible.

- **Social Backing:** People look to those around them to guide their decisions, especially their own peers. This is a critical part of influence. It's much easier to influence someone when they've heard something positive about you. This makes acting with integrity more important than ever. Every decision you make can either take away from or contribute to your image as an influencer.

- **Commitment and Consistency:** People strive for consistency in their commitments. To influence others, gently encourage them to publicly commit. People are more likely to follow through with action when they say "yes." It's important to know how to get others excited about your ideas. Enthusiasm is contagious, so if you have hopes to influence or persuade other people, learn how to cultivate enthusiasm in yourself, and then see how it pays off.

- **Authentic Connection:** Taking the time to foster true connections with the people you're working with is worth the time and effort, since people tend to favor those that are like them. Even something as small as having the same name or growing up in the same city can play a role in how someone receives you. Finding basic connections and establishing those with others is a fantastic way to influence others in a positive way. With this common ground established, you will find everything about influencing others easier.

- **Authority- backed experience:** Most people respect authority, especially when it comes to experts in any given field. Testimonials from proven experts or their students are one way that your level of influence increases. If you aren't an expert in your field yet, make it your mission to become one, and people will have more respect for your ideas. Take the time to research and prove yourself.

The Importance of Rapport in Influence:

Rapport is an essential ingredient in an influential relationship, and refers to a state of shared understanding between you and a group or individual. From this baseline of rapport, easier and greater conversation is possible. To say it another way, rapport is simply getting along with and having things in common with people, and as we've said a few times in the book already, that is at the center of all effective persuasion. At times, this level of rapport happens without effort and leads to great friendships that may last a lifetime. But you can learn to build rapport with just about anyone, as long as you know how.

The Benefits of Rapport:

Rapport is something that humans create on an instinctive level, as a way to avoid conflict and create positive, beneficial bonds with others. Most humans will avoid conflict instinctively, usually without even being aware that they do it. In this section, we will go over some methods for building rapport, particularly with people you've just met. This quality is crucial in our personal and professional lives alike. So, what are some benefits to knowing how to build rapport with others?

- **Better Career Chances:** Having the skill of knowing how to bu. rapport will increase your opportunities on a professional scale since employees will always choose to hire the person they think will fit in well with their current employees. On the other side of things, a business person who is pleasant to be around and easy to talk to will have a better time finding quality employees. In addition to this, knowing how to build rapport will give you a higher level of influence over people you work with or customers you see on a day to day basis.

- **Better Personal Relations:** Personal relationships rely heavily on a sense of rapport between the two parties, even those who have never heard the term. This involves a deeper connection and a higher awareness of the needs of the other person. Since the essence of any valuable relationship is trust and closeness, focusing on rapport is a must with your loved ones and friends. Before you move on to rapport-building with people you've never met, you can practice the techniques on people you already know.

- **An Easier time Starting Conversations:** Many people find it hard to start conversations with someone they don't know. You may end up feeling awkward, or speechless because you don't know what to say next. In building rapport, you learn how to match your own vibe with that of another person. In effect, this is a skill that allows you to steer interactions in a more positive direction. Regardless of how nervous or stressed out you may feel at that moment, learning to decrease your own tension will allow for more rapport to grow.

All of the above reasons are great incentives to learn how to develop rapport with people, especially those you wish to influence. In essence, this refers to the ability to "break the ice" when you first meet someone, no matter who they are. We can maintain and create rapport on a subconscious level by matching ourselves up to the signals of another person, including the movements of their bodies, tones, and facial expressions. One only has to observe two close friends chatting to see this phenomenon in action. So, what are some foolproof methods for developing this valuable skill?

ctics for Building Rapport with Others:

how to Listen: Perhaps the most important element for building rapport and being an influential person in general, is listening. Learn how to listen to the words another is saying and search for circumstances or experiences that you share and can relate to them on. A keen listener will always find subjects to talk about since they were paying close attention to the words of the other person, and this is always appreciated.

- **Use Humor:** People are much more likely to respond favorably to a person who makes them laugh or smile, so learning how to inject humor into a situation is a valuable skill to have. When you laugh with another person, effortless harmony is created. You can start by joking about a circumstance or situation that is happening at that moment, or a joke about yourself. Definitely avoid making fun of others, however, since people who do this are harder to trust, especially those you have just met.

- **Stick to Safe Subjects:** When you first meet someone, sticking to safe subjects or "small talk" is recommended, since you don't know them yet. This could include talking about experiences that you both had, travel, or the weather at that moment. Don't ask questions in a way that is too direct and lay off on only talking about yourself. Keep in mind that conversations should always be a two-way street, with plenty of back and forth.

- **Stay Aware of Nonverbal Language:** Always pay attention to your nonverbal language is important for building rapport. This includes holding eye contact more than half the time (but not too much), and maintaining a relaxed posture. You should also face the person you're talking to, since this indicates that you are listening to them. Appropriate body language is one of the most crucial aspects of building rapport with others. Most influence happens on a nonverbal level, whereas people are harder to persuade using words alone. When a mismatch happens between what we say with our voice and what we show with our nonverbal cues, the person is more likely to believe the nonverbal cues. This makes a relaxing and open stance all the more important. Don't cross your legs or arms, since this indicates an aggressive state of mind. You should also remember to smile.

- **Repeating:** In addition to matching and focusing on nonverbal cues, we should also try to match our words with theirs. This involves reflecting on what they say, asking questions for clarification, and repeating back what they said using our own words. This proves that you are actively listening to what they say and goes a long way to establishing common ground and similarities between you and that person.

- **Keep Empathy in Mind:** Show that you understand where the other person is coming from by relating to what they're saying with personal experiences of your own. You can also ask interested questions about the other person to show that you have empathy for what they are saying. Show that you care about what they say, and this will lead to them responding more favorably to you and the conversation as a whole.

- **Pay Attention to your Tone:** How you speak is also an important element for rapport-building. When someone feels tense or nervous, they have a tendency to speak faster, adding a stressful element to the conversation. Try varying your volume, pitch, and tone to come across as friendlier and more open. Talk in a soft and slow manner, with a low tone. People have a tendency to trust you more when you speak with confidence, and taking your time with what you say is the perfect way to display this.

- **Use their Name:** Using someone's name as you talk to them will help them see you as a polite person. It will also help you to remember their name, since forgetting someone's name can kill rapport early on in a conversation. In addition to this, ask them open ended questions, rather than simple yes/no questions. This will help the conversation flow.

- **Give Reasons why you Agree:** Agreeing with someone is a good way to get rapport going, especially if you nod to show you're listening and make sounds that indicate agreement, but you should go into detail about why you agree with them. This will build on their ideas and keep the conversation fresh and flowing. On the other hand, if something comes up that you aren't sure about, don't be afraid to openly state that you don't know, and ask interested questions to clarify. Most people will be happy to explain any confusion to you in this situation as long as you are humble about it.

Building rapport essentially means that you are including the other person but not intimidating them. Remember that the best person to have a conversation with is someone who is interested, yet relaxed. Another important key here is to maintain an attitude of non-judgment. Forget about any assumptions or prejudice you may have had about whoever you're speaking with. Don't be afraid to give them a compliment, and do your best to remain polite and stay away from conflict or criticism. If you follow all of these tips, you should be building rapport with people in no time!

Chapter 4: The Fourth Law- Simple Body Language Signs that Influence

We already went over some basic body language tips in the last chapter to help you build rapport and, as a consequence, help you with your level of influence. So, let's go into some more detail about body language and how it will help you with persuasion.

The 4th Law of Influence: Simple Body Language Signs that Influence

Simple actions that can have a positive effect on others:

- **Smiling**: A genuine smile tells the other person you are warm, confident and approachable. Studies show that a person feels more favorable toward another if that person is smiling, rather than frowning or looking neutral. Smiling is a habit that makes you feel happier, in general, and also becomes more natural with time, the more you practice it.

- **Matching**: You can have more influence if you match yourself up with the other person's movements: This helps build rapport through establishing a common ground. Shows your similarities as you mimic others. People will naturally observe this, but remember to be subtle and not too over the top with it.

- **Nodding**: Nodding while someone is talking shows you are engaged and listening. So many people are used to people being distracted while they are talking, this is a simple way to show you care. Also, you can nod while you are talking to help influence the person to agree with you. It is no guarantee, but when you nod while asking a question, people often unknowingly nod as well, signifying they are agreeing with what you are saying.

- **Standing**: Adopting a posture of standing helps you feel powerful and confident. This is useful when giving presentations. Just make sure not to stand over anyone, as that is a sign of a threat to most people.

- **Head Positioning**:Tilting your head or body toward someone shows you are interested. If you make others feel important then you have the opportunity to positively influence them. Also, having your head pointed toward the person speaking shows that you care what they are saying, whereas looking around indicates disinterest.

- **Feet Positioning**: This is a factor that many may forget to consider, but it's very important and helpful when it comes to influence and persuasion. Much like head positioning, the position of your feet can also have a subconscious effect on someone. Pointing your feet towards someone shows you are interested. It is a positive signal that builds trust.

Communicating on an interpersonal level has more to do with just the meaning of spoken words. Human communication is vast and complex, and also contains messages on an implicit level, whether you are aware of it or not. These messages are conveyed through body language. Body language includes your gestures, facial expressions, and also the way you use your voice. In addition to this, the amount of distance between you and another person communicates nonverbal cues.

How does Nonverbal Communication Work?

Body language signals give extra information, along with clues to meaning, in conversation. Messages that are given through body language let you:

- **Modify and Reinforce:** Some people nod along with someone when they agree or to say "yes", while they will shrug to show a neutral or uncertain position. A shrug could mean something completely different, however, when combined with a sad facial expression.

- **Define Relationships:** The way people communicate using body language says a lot about how they feel for each other. Displays of affection, obviously, show a closer relationship, and there are distinct differences between platonic displays and non-platonic displays. They also provide important feedback as to where you stand with someone.

- **Transmit Emotional Information:** Body language is perhaps the most important tool for transmitting emotional information that can't always be conveyed with words. Someone may say one thing, but if their body language, tone, and facial expression tells a different story, we will know it's not true. It's also used to transmit feedback and show someone how you feel about what they are saying.

- **Directing Communication:** Nonverbal cues can be useful for showing someone when you're done talking or when you have an idea you want to share. There are also plenty of gestures that communicate specific ideas, based on your culture.

Is Body Language a Language you can Learn?

Plenty of books exist on the subject of body language which show the subject as a language that you can teach and learn. In other words if each small expression of the face and movement of the body were studied and documented, we could understand each other's true intentions and feelings. Although this may be true, in a sense, successfully interpreting signals of body language isn't all that easy or simple. Nonverbal cues and body language is not the type of language that has objective meanings for signals. The language is driven and influenced heavily by specific context, including where it happens, the people partaking in communication, and the culture they are from.

Nodding your head, for example, may seem to have an obvious meaning on the surface; saying "yes." But think about the difference between nodding at someone you don't know, and nodding at your co-worker during a meeting. Communicating on an interpersonal level is far more complex since it isn't always possible to correctly interpret expressions or gestures on their own. Body language involves an entire, nuanced pack of micro-expressions, including postures, movements of the eyes and hands, and other gestures that accompany verbal communication.

How Culture Plays a Role in this:

Most people have already learned to interpret body language while developing and growing up. This is a natural and accepted part of the way we communicate with each other, and most people use the language on a regular basis and know how to read it, as well, on a subconscious level. Due to this, it isn't always easy to interpret nonverbal cues in a conscious manner, but if you can get your brain to quiet down and stop over-thinking it, there's a fair chance that you will understand what someone was trying to communicate to you. However, nonverbal cues are very specific to different cultures.

Specific Cues that Vary by Culture:

- **Excitement:** There is a stereotype out there about Italian culture that says that they wave their hands a lot, talk louder than others, and use large gestures. In their culture, they tend to show enthusiasm in a way that is more obvious than other countries, such as the UK. In countries like the US or UK, it may be harder to interpret what is being said, since they rely on more subtle cues. But, just within the country of Italy, there are variations and exceptions this.

- **Thumbs Up:** In most English speaking countries, holding your thumb up shows that you approve of something, whereas in other countries, it can be considered very rude. These areas are the Middle East (some parts), Italy, and Greece.

- **The "OK" Symbol:** Making the "OK" sign with your hand signals approval or being alright with something. However, in Japan, it is the symbol for money. In some Middle Eastern countries, it's seen as very rude or threatening.

What we say through our body language is just as important as our words, or even more so. All of the above, and more, prove why it's important to learn the ropes of body language. If you are traveling to a foreign country, it's a good idea to look up these cultural differences ahead of time. What you communicate with nonverbal cues plays a huge role in the conversation and the way it will go, so it's worth learning about, especially if you are interested in influence and persuasion.

What if there is a Mismatch between Speech and Cues?

Keep in mind that people tend to have far less control over what their body language is communicating than which words they choose. Since body language relies more on emotions, it's an instinctive reaction, not a conscious one. This means that if the two seem to be contradicting each other, it's safer to trust the body language instead of the words. Even someone showing a lack of body language could be significant, and signal that they might be attempting to hide feelings.

Different Types of Body Language to Recognize for Influence:

If you want to master influence, you need to know how to read the body language of others, and also send the signals you want to send to people you speak with. Different types of nonverbal cues include:

- **Posture:** This refers to the way you sit or stand, and whether your posture is "open" or "closed". An example of closed posture would be sitting with your arms and legs crossed, while an open posture would indicate relaxed limbs.

- **Kinesics:** This words refers to the motions of the body, including head shaking, nodding, or gestures of the hands.

- **Vocal Patterns:** Apart from speech, there are telling signals in the words used which rely on how fast one talks, the tone they use, and their pitch. These refer to something known as para-language.

- **Eye Contact:** One of the most obvious and noticeable of all body language cues, the way someone holds (or doesn't hold) eye contact often indicates how much they trust or are trustworthy. Trouble holding eye contact could also signal shyness.

- **Expressions:** This is also an obvious one, but someone's facial expressions communicate a lot about what they are feeling, including frowning, smiling, and blinking.

- **Proximity:** How close or far away someone stands or sits next to you, or while talking to you, is a reliable indication of intimacy or a wish for intimacy.

But body language isn't just limited to the points listed above. When someone blinks more, it can be a significant indication that they are nervous or tired, and sweating and heart rate also indicates someone's state of mind and feelings. Being aware of all of this can help you accurately gauge how well you are relating with someone, and noticing these signals will help you be a better communicator and influencer.

Chapter 5: The Fifth Law- The Communication Skills Needed to Influence

The words you choose to use play a large role in how persuasive and influential you are. Effectively mastering spoken and verbal communication relies on a few different factors and can't be pinned down to just one aspect. How clear you are with your speaking, your ability to stay focused and calm, along with your level of politeness and etiquette will all go to show your adeptness at communicating. This chapter is intended to help you start paying more attention to all of this, since your spoken cues are important to your level of influence. You must know how to gauge whether your messages are coming across as you hope. Let's take a look at some helpful examples of this.

The 5th Law of Influence: The Communication Skills Needed to Influence

- **Focus on the Future:** You have to do this without being pushy. Example: "We will" instead "we'll see." When you speak with future tense it helps people know that you are moving forward.

- **Speak their Language**: Similar to mimicking body language, the same can be done with people's speech. If they talk fast, you can talk fast. If they talk slow, you can slow down. If they use simple speech, use simple speech. If they are direct, be direct. This will help create a connection based on a similarity.

- **Avoid Spacer Words:** Words like "um" and "uh" should be avoided. Pausing a conversation with these words loses your credibility and shows a lack of clear focus and decision.

- **Express your Opinion with Hesitancy**: especially if it is against what they believe. When trying to overcome an objection, the simple phrase, "this is what I used to believe, but this is what I believe now," can work to ease any potential conflict and help create assurance for the other person.

- **Repeat**: Repeat back what the other person said. This shows that you are engaged and listening and that you comprehend what they said. Don't do it too often, but when appropriate for the conversation. When others feel listened to, if establishes a connection.

- **Acknowledge Credibility:** this helps create mutual respect even when opinions or choices differ. When you can acknowledge someone else's opinion, it naturally tells the other person that you accept them, even if you don't agree. This opens the door for further discussion and influence down the road.

- **Dress Code and Communication**: Often times, the way you dress will help influence not only others, but yourself. Dressing up can actually enhance your communication skills because when you dress nice and feel confident, your words reflect that. While what you wear isn't a direct interaction with someone, it can certainly affect how you use your communication skills and how others perceive you.

Initial Communication with Others:

We've all heard the saying that first impressions are the most important of all. This may be an exaggeration, since people can change their minds later, but the first few moments of an interaction are very important. Every person has certain norms in mind or expectations about the way first meetings should go. If it turns out their expectations are not met or simply clash with those of another, it's highly unlikely that verbal communication will go well. Here are a few things you should do every time you meet someone, no matter who they are:

- **A Handshake:** Be sure to be firm, with this, but not overly firm.

- **Eye Contact:** Remember that you should hold eye contact a bit more than half the time.

- **An Introduction:** Complete with name and (if the occasion is formal) last name.

- **Neutral Conversation:** Stick to safe topics, such as the weather, your trip, or other common niceties.

- **A Friendly Expression:** A smile is a better choice than a neutral face, which could indicate boredom.

Some of these may seem obvious, but it's easy to forget at least one of the above when you are distracted, tired, or busy. Although you can salvage a poor first impression, it's better to not have to worry about that at all in the first place.

The Art of Reinforcement in Communication:

Using words that are positive and encouraging in addition to encouraging gestures (like nodding of the head) and friendly expressions, with plenty of eye contact, will almost certainly make the person you're speaking with feel more comfortable with you, as well as open. Using positive and encouraging reinforcement will:

- **Encourage Participation:** This is especially relevant in group situations, but showing open communication proves that you want others to join in on the conversation. Having an inclusive attitude like this helps you come across as a respectable person to others.

- **Show Interest:** Making sure you remain open in communication shows that you are interested in what others are saying or wish to say, and can contribute to the developing of new friendships or partnerships. No one is interested in a person who doesn't show interest in others, so keep this in mind for the future.

Knowing how to Listen Effectively:

Listening effectively (also known as active listening) is a skill that is important for communication. It's far too common that people simply wait for their turn to talk, instead of truly listening. Here are the steps for developing this useful skill:

- Get in a Prepared State of Mind for Listening.

- Stay Open-minded, but also focused on the Words.

- Avoid becoming Distracted.

- Try not to Judge, and stay Objective.

- Don't think of What you will Say Next until the Person is Done.

The Importance of Questioning during Listening:

Knowing how to ask open questions during conversation is also a useful skill. Using questioning in the correct way can help you:

- Begin a Conversation.
- Receive Valuable Information.
- Gauge the Understanding of Another.
- Include Others in the Talk.
- Indicate Interest.
- Obtain Agreement or Support.

Avoiding Closed Questions for True Communication:

A closed question is a question that can only be answered in one words (usually "no" or "yes"). This severely limits the potential for where a conversation can go. This specific type of communication usually leaves control of the talk in the hands of the person doing the questioning, and thus is not inclusive or constructive. Sure, it's useful for getting specific answers, but as far as getting to know someone or developing an influential relationship, it's better to use open language and questions.

Using Open Questions for True Communication:

Open language and questions, on the other hand, open up the possibilities for a conversation, since they give opportunities for someone to elaborate. These questions may be a bit more complicated, but that's the point. Asking questions that cannot be answered with just one word show that you want to engage with the person you are asking.

Clarifying and Thinking in Spoken Communication:

Thinking about what someone just said is the act of reflecting on their words to indicate understanding or seek understanding. This is a tactic used widely in the field of counseling, but can be used in everyday life, as well.

Thinking on someone's words has to do with summing up what they said in your own way, to prove that you truly absorbed what they meant. This is useful because:

- It Enables you to Make sure you Understand.

- You can Provide Feedback on the Person's Communication.

- It Indicates Respect and Interest in their Words.

Using Summarizing in Spoken Communication:

Knowing how to effectively summarize the words of another person is also a highly useful skill. This involves going over a recap of the main gist of what they just said. This allows you to make sure that you are both on the same page, trade information, and more. Summarizing what you took to be a person's point of view shows that you are actually listening and taking an active part in the conversation, not just being a passive observer.

How to End Conversations:

The way you close communication is important, as well, since this will determine how the person remembers the talk and you. There are plenty of subtle cues (and plenty of overt ones) that can be used to close a conversation. This could be standing up, starting to walk away, or not making eye contact. All of this shows that the person wishes to end the talk. If you do this too quickly or abruptly, you could come across as brash or not considerate enough to let the person finish their thoughts. During the closing of a conversation is when you should make plans for the future.

Skills for Communication that Improve your Level of Influence:

Standing out in the crowd is crucial for becoming an influential person. If you listen to the average, everyday conversations happening around you, most of them won't be very exciting. For this reason, having stronger skills of persuasion and influence means breaking this trend. Words are some of our most valuable tools as human beings, they can create businesses, start a romance, or even bring kingdoms crashing down. Knowing how to use them to your benefit is a must. Here are a few key ways you can begin improving yours, starting today:

- **Don't be Cliché:** It's too easy to fall into the "standard" when it comes to talking, especially with strangers. When someone asks you how you are, try not to answer them with just another cliché answer that they have already heard a million times. Try to tell them what is actually going on that day. Whether you are nervous about an upcoming test, or excited for a job interview, you should tell the person who asks. When you break the familiar mold, people have a tendency to listen more closely and find you more interesting.

- **Express yourself:** Instead of using mundane words like "good" or "bad", you should actually express yourself with more detail. For example, "That service was amazingly fantastic". Being more expressive automatically comes across as confident, heightens your level of influence, and works in many situations, either professional or personal.

- **Don't be Afraid to Ask:** When you want something, you should learn to ask for it. Too many people tip toe through life, too afraid to go after their desires, and they end up waiting on the sidelines. Think about how many first dates started with someone being too afraid to ask, and then ended in marriage. This is an extreme example, but you get the gist of what this means.

- **Be Funny:** When you inject humor into everyday interactions, such as a request for a receptionist to send an email for you, you automatically make the person you're speaking with open up and relax. The interaction goes from something boring and forgettable, to an enjoyable experience and instantly breaks the ice.

In order to be someone who is influential, you should learn to stand out. In order to get noticed, be persuasive, and stir up interest in other people, you should pay attention to the way you speak in everyday life. Not only will you cheer up the people around you, but it will make you feel more confident, as well.

Chapter 6: The Sixth Law- How to Influence without Words

We already covered a bit on the topic of listening in an earlier chapter, but this subject deserves some more detail and depth to it. You would be surprised at how many people assume that influence is all about speaking, and how much of it is truly about knowing how to listen to who you're talking to.

The 6th Law of Influence: How to Influence Without Words

Listening is the key to influencing others, not speaking.

- **Why is Listening Important?** Because when you are listening to someone, it makes them feel important and that what they say and what they do matters. Listening is based on a giving mindset and is opposite of how most humans are wired, which is to focus on ourselves first. When people feel heard and they feel good about themselves, they are likely to attribute those good feelings to the person that helped stir them up. When you listen to someone that is actually what you do.

- **Hearing vs. Really Listening:** There is a distinct difference between listening and hearing something vs. actively listening and engaging. Hearing means that you are aware, on some level, that someone is speaking, but you aren't fully involved or engaged in what they're saying or paying much attention. Real, active listening means you are focused on their words, looking straight at them, and absorbing their ideas.

In this chapter, we will cover details on how to actively listen (make eye contact, face toward the person, acknowledge their words, ask questions, be accepting and non-judgmental, etc.) At the end of the day listening is what builds connection and is one of the strongest ways to positively influence others.

Tips for Better Listening:

Not everyone is naturally good at listening. You may zone out of the conversation, find yourself growing distracted, or even find that you have trouble looking at them as they speak. You might also notice that you just wait for your turn to speak instead of absorbing their ideas. This isn't helpful for building rapport or influence. Here are some tips to help you become better at listening:

- **It's a Win/Win Situation:** A lot of people have a hard time paying attention fully and listening in a conversation because they don't think there is much to gain from it. However, the better you get at this skill, the more you get it back from the other person, which leads to deeper and more meaningful connections. If you truly pay attention to the person, and try to add something of value to the talk, you will receive the same in return.

- **Relay the Info Later:** A useful tip for learning to truly tune in to a talk is telling yourself to remember it so you can relate the information to another person later. Even if you won't actually do this, it helps you stay alert and curious to the subject at hand. Then you can forget about what you were planning to say after the person is done and truly focus, leading to more quality conversations.

- **No Smart Phones:** Surfing your electronic vice as you attempt to listen to another person is about as counterproductive as it can get. You will definitely miss what they are saying, at least partially. In addition to that, many people see this as rude and will instantly stop being interested in the conversation once someone pulls their phone out. Resist the urge to check your email, keep your phone in your pocket, and wait until you're done with the conversation to look something up.

- **Don't Assume, Ask**: Instead of assuming what the other person meant, when you aren't certain, ask for clarification. No one is a mind reader, meaning that you probably won't be able to interpret every single thing they wish to convey. Next time you notice that you are assuming something about another person's thoughts, pause your reasoning and switch to questioning instead of assuming.

- **Keep a Clear Head**: Getting plenty of exercise and fresh air may not seem like it's related to being a good communicator (and listener), but keeping up with a conversation is much easier when you are not foggy or tired. You can instantly boost your mental energy and clarity by taking a short walk or getting some air by opening a window. Making sure you get exercise on a regular basis will also help you with your energy levels and focus.

- **Be Singularly Focused**: Meaning that when you engage in listening, that is all you're doing at that moment. Resist the urge to interrupt the person, and don't immediately jump in to contribute your solution to an issue at hand (some people will find this difficult). Just remember to stay in that moment and fully listen to whoever you are engaging with. Allow them to decide when they are done talking, and then when you're sure they're done, you can contribute your two cents. Many times, a listening ear is all that someone needs for them to come to a conclusion on their own.

- **Be Transparent**: When it comes to truly listening, don't be afraid to be upfront about whatever is going on with you in that moment. Maybe you're exhausted, nervous about a test coming up, or in a hurry. Make sure you communicate this in order to avoid misunderstandings. If you need to take a break from the conversation to grab a bite to eat, let them know that, as well. Real communication happens when people are honest and upfront with each other. When you are out of energy for listening, step back and return to the conversation later.

As stated in the beginning of the chapter, influence has everything to do with being able to listen to people and help them feel heard and appreciated. When the time comes, the person you listened to will be happy to repay the favor by lending an ear to you when you need it, and they will also be a lot more receptive to your ideas and influence.

Chapter 7: The Seventh Law- The Keys to Positive Persuasion

Positivity is an important aspect of being an influential person. Negative influence is never successful for very long, and having someone reluctantly agree with your influence will not be beneficial for you in the long run. It's better to attain positive, enthusiastic agreement, which shows commitment. Being a more positive person helps you in all interpersonal relationships and goals.

7th Law of Influence: The Keys to Positive Persuasion

- **Persuasion is not Manipulation:** Manipulation is forceful, and has a highly negative connotation. The word manipulation implies that there is deceit involved in the arrangement, whereas persuasion is getting people to do what is in their best interest but that also benefits you.

- **How Reciprocation Benefits Everyone:** When you are kind to someone and do favors for them, they often feel as though they should pay you back. This does not have to be a negative, obligated sensation, but can instead be something they are happy to do. Reciprocity compels others to act.

- **Persistence:** Another key to being a persuasive person is to keep asking for what you want and demonstrating value at the same time. Nagging is when you bother someone about something repeatedly, effective persuasion is when you make polite requests but also give something in return for what you request.

General Principles of Persuasion:

- **Interest:** You have to be interested in the other person to persuade them. If they can sense that you are stuck on whatever your objective is, and only see them as a means to an end, it likely won't go well. Try, instead, to see the person you are engaging with.

- **Genuine Appreciation:** Sincerely compliment others, this builds trust and shows that you see value in them as a person outside of the favor you wish for or task you are trying to achieve. You don't have to be over the top with it, but simply noticing when someone has done something well and pointing it out will usually be very appreciated.

- **Set Expectations:** Setting clear cut expectations keeps you in control of the conversation and what happens as you move forward. This also decreases the other person's fear of the unknown. Instead of waiting until the other person has to ask out of confusion, simply make things as clear as possible from the beginning. This will avoid potential conflicts and will also help everyone involved focus better on whatever task is at hand.

- **Utilize Imagery in Persuasion:** Use images. Mental images in the minds of others can be a powerful way to persuade others. Learn to paint pictures with your words to get people more interested in what you are saying, and invested in it. If you aren't good at this yet, find ways to improve.

- **Focus on Rapport:** Use the tips we gave you earlier in the book to effectively build rapport. Find common connection points and always come across as genuine and certain, instead of nervous or tense. This creates an environment that is relaxed and allows the other person to open up to you on a real level.

- **Confidence and Calm:** Stay calm in the face of stressful situations and always assert your confidence in a humble, respectful manner. These types of people always end up being the ones that others refer to for authority, and it establishes your influence and persuasion abilities.

- **Powerful Communication:** Use communication skills, both verbal and nonverbal, to transfer positive energy. Do that through eye contact, touch, laughter, excitement in responses or active listening. When a person can tell that you are engaged with what they're saying and truly care, they will feel better about you as a person and open up more. This fosters the perfect relationship for motivation and influence.

More Persuasion Techniques for Positive Influence:

The entire point of negotiation is knowing how to inspire others to act. One of the key factors in successful negotiation is techniques for persuasion, and knowing how to persuade people is at the center of this process. Giving encouragement to others to open up is a good way to persuade people, and it all depends on which approach you decide you use. Learning about different techniques can also help you recognize when someone is attempting to persuade you. Being able to recognize this will keep you in a clear mindset about your own best interests.

In many different negotiations, people assume that that are negative motivating factors at play, such as greed or avarice. Although these are naturally present in many negotiations, it isn't a way to build lasting, influential relationships, and they don't have to be the main focus, at all. Many different techniques exist out there for effective persuasion, and these positive tips are a good place to start:

- **Reinforcing in a Positive Way:** Everyone wants to be well-liked by their peers, and one of the best techniques for persuading others is using conditioning that is based on positive reinforcement. In any situation that requires persuasion, there are plenty of issues that should be set in place before the main negotiation takes place. You should reinforce someone's association with you as early on as you can.

    Showing them appreciation by smiling each time they do something for you, some type of gesture of appreciation, or a sincere handshake, will all contribute to reinforcing how they perform. Once you begin to show that you like this person and what they are doing, they are likely to continue seeking your approval through these cues you've given.

    Watch out for the trap of trying to be liked no matter what. Although it's perfectly natural for humans to wish for others to like them, when it comes to persuasion, it's important to keep your confidence and self-esteem. This will help you stay the one doing the influencing, and keep it positive. If you start feeling uncertain, it's too easy to be swayed or veer off course. Make sure you always stand up for yourself when it's necessary.

- **Staying Truly Respectful**: Someone can be highly persuasive when they overtly show that they respect the expertise of another. Showing that you recognize their strong qualities and wish to borrow an idea from them is a great way to help influence them. The idea of this strategy is to help the person go into a mode of speaking where they start acting as a mentor or coach and give you the information you're seeking.

  As soon as this has happened, you can either accept what they are saying, or adjust it, to come up with the best plan that works for both of you. This is a great way to learn more about the person while injecting your influence into the situation. They will also feel more favorably toward you when you appeal to their expertise, knowledge, or power.

- **Using Success as a Motivator**: Every person out there in the world wishes to be successful. At times, this can become even more crucial than the issue at hand. A well-used technique for persuasion is to recognize the success of another person, and then ask them if you can join in on the result. This may require that you put your ego aside a bit, but it can have powerful results since most people wish to be recognized and appreciated.

  This will, in turn, help that person feel more favorable about you and create a positive association with you in their mind. This is a great way to build rapport, along with a relationship where you can persuade and influence that person in a way that is mutually beneficial.

How to Attain and Maintain Positivity:

Who in this world doesn't want to be happy? If you asked the average person, I'm sure most of them would list a happy life as their goal. It's a positive aspect in being able to influence and persuade others, and also to have a great impact on the world, in general. How is passion related to positive thinking?

- **The Importance of Passion in Positivity:** The principle in positive thinking says that in order to sustain your energy levels and positivity, get interested in something. It's impossible to stay excited and enthusiastic about something if you don't actually believe in it. As a result, you won't be able to motivate others to get committed or enthusiastic in a project if you seem humdrum about it all. Find something that ignites excitement within you, which will be contagious to those around you.

- **Passion Contributes to Focus:** Finding and pursuing your passion will help sustain you through the difficult times. In addition to this, passion helps sustain mental focus and clarity. Whenever you find that your old passion is fading out, you have to find ways to renew it, by either getting re-interested in a subject or finding a new one altogether.

- **Finding a New Interest:** Exploring a new passion creates excitement and positive energy. That positive energy can sustain you and actually aid you in creating a positive mindset. Once this flow of energy starts going, it builds upon itself and keeps growing and growing. What is that interest you've always wanted to get into but haven't had the time? Now is the time to pursue it. Even if it isn't related directly to your career goals, that excitement of something new will bleed over into the rest of your life.

- **Brainstorm:** Maybe it isn't so easy to come up with a new passion to explore. If this applies to you, it's time to do some soul searching and find out what your highest excitement is. Try to find the link between doing something you love and what that means to you. Explore what you like and what excites you. On a deeper level, finding and pursuing a life purpose will be the ultimate test in positive thinking.

- **The Importance of True Purpose in Life:** Just like a hobby or passion, a purpose provides a useful challenge and something that can give you massive positive energy and enthusiasm. Without a direction to direct our energy, it's easy to become uninspired, bored, and hopeless. Finding something to give yourself to helps imbue life with purpose and meaning. This makes you a more positive person and, as a consequence, a better influencer.

- **Being Involved in Something Bigger:** Living in pursuit of your purpose will allow you to do something bigger than yourself. By living for a purpose you will be able to serve others, which will help you maintain your perspective, build your faith and confidence, and sustain positive expectations of good results. Rather than feeling rootless and separate from everyone and everything around you, you will feel like you truly belong in this world, connecting to it through your passion.

Finding and living on purpose is the best way to develop the good habit of positive thinking. We have already stated plenty about the fact that people are more easily influenced by a person that they actually like. Being positive means you will make friends easier and that people will simply enjoy you as a person more. This means that focusing on passion, which fuels positivity, is a great place to start on your journey. It combines all these principles in this book and gives them a place to be applied and lived out. So, be encouraged to seek and discover your purpose.

Conclusion

Thank you again for purchasing this book!

I hope this book was able to help you to learn about how important influence is, along with productive ways you can use it to improve your life personally and professionally. Having control over your own life is a goal that everyone has. And in a world where everything is related to and dependent on other things, we can only control ourselves. Working on this is the only way to develop genuine influence. The closer other people are, physically and personally, to us, the more we can influence them.

The next step is to think about influence as a way that you can help others, and use some of the methods outlined in this book to achieve your goals of persuasion. While attempting to control others requires a conscious intention, influence does not. This is why the capacity to influence people is far more important than the capacity for control. Simply being the person that you are means that you are always using your power of influence. This means that the ultimate choice lies in the way you will exert your influence, and whether it will be a positive or negative thing. Hopefully, this book was able to help you use it in a positive manner and empower your life, and those around you, as a result.

Finally, if you enjoyed this book, then I'd like to ask you for a favor, would you be kind enough to leave a review for this book on Amazon? It'd be greatly appreciated!

Thank you and good luck!

P.S-Don't forget to check out your FREE BONUS on the next page! You won't want to miss out on it!

Also check out my other books from the "7 Laws" Series on success and personal growth on the last page!

FREE BONUS E-BOOK!

Get Success Results:

220 Principles That the Successful Use to Become Wildly Successful and How You Can Too

Learn the secrets and habits of the most successful people in the world and how you too can develop the right habits for success so you can live the life you've always wanted…

http://shapleighpublishing.com/GetSuccessResultsEbook/

OTHER BOOKS IN THE "7 LAWS" SERIES

Check out the current and the upcoming books in Brian Cagneey's "7 Laws" series on personal development and success!

amazon.com/author/briancagneey

The 7 Laws Of Habits: Using Habits To Achieve Success, Happiness, And Anything You Want!

The 7 Laws Of Motivation: Explode Your Motivation And Create A Mindset Built For Success

The 7 Laws of Happiness: Using The Power of Happiness to Create Amazing Results in Life!

The 7 Laws of Productivity: 10X Your Success with Focus, Time Management, Self-Discipline, And Action.

The 7 Laws of Fear: Break What's Holding You Back and Turn Fear into Confidence.

The 7 Laws of Confidence: Feel Unstoppable, Destroy Doubt, And Accomplish Your Biggest Goals.

The 7 Laws of Focus: Focus: The #1 Secret for Excellence, Productivity and Radical Results.

The 7 Laws of Leadership: Develop Yourself, Influence Others and People Will Follow.

The 7 Laws of Communication: The Secrets of Being Comfortable, Confident, And Unforgettable with Anyone!

The 7 Laws of Self-Discipline: Become Strong, Become Confident and Create Your Success

The 7 Laws of Coaching: Powerful Coaching Skills That Will Predict Your Team's Success

The 7 Laws of Mental Toughness: Mental Training for Success Using Emotional Intelligence, Grit, and Mental Toughness Training

The 7 Laws of Positive Thinking: Positive Energy Through Self Help: Using The Power of Belief to Destroy Negativity

amazon.com/author/briancagneey

THE 7 LAWS OF

Brian Cagneey is the author of the well-known "7 Laws" book series on personal development. His books cover a wide range of topics including personal growth, habits, self-discipline, happiness, success, communication, leadership, coaching, motivation, confidence, fear, productivity, and focus.

Brian's mission is to renew people's minds and to help everyday, ordinary people become positive, successful, and mission driven. His passion for writing is fueled by the desire to see as many people as possible not just survive their life but thrive and excel.

Brian is an avid student of the laws of success. His beliefs on accomplishment are not based on theory, but real life practice. Brian knows that wisdom and knowledge are only half of the equation, the other half of success is taking massive amounts of action over a sustained period of time.

"Anyone can succeed with the ultimate principle of success: small, consistent action over a long period of time. If anyone can master that law through focus, self-discipline and confidence, there isn't anything that's impossible to accomplish."

Check out the other book in the "7 Laws" series today!

amazon.com/author/briancagneey

Printed in Great Britain
by Amazon